Home Sweet Apartment

Home Sweet Apartment

GETTING RIGHTSIZED
IN OUR SEVENTIES

Daniel Carlson

ISBN-13: 9781547221233
ISBN-10: 1547221232

Table of Contents

Dedication

⁓

This is dedicated to Bonnie who, for
more than fifty years, has been my wife,
my friend and my fellow-traveller

… I get Misty just holding your hand …

Introduction

∽

IN 1963, PRESIDENT JOHN F. Kennedy threw his "hat over the wall."

Speaking at the dedication of the Aerospace Medical Health Center in San Antonio, Texas, he emphasized his commitment to the exploration of space, and his goal of landing a man on the moon before the end of the decade. Though many doubted whether this was even possible, he said the United States would meet this challenge the same way two young Irish lads who, while exploring the countryside, overcame an obstacle blocking their way. Stopped momentarily by a high orchard wall, they hesitated only a moment before they agreed on a solution; they threw their hats over the wall. Now there was no other option ... they had to find a way over the wall.

By using this particular metaphor, President Kennedy clearly stated his vision while acknowledging that the space program would be moving into uncharted territory. And, of course, the first United States astronauts landed on the moon in 1969.

In early 2017, my wife, Bonnie, and I threw our hats over the wall by selling our house and moving into an apartment. This choice was not nearly as momentous as Kennedy's plan for NASA, of course, but for us it had the potential to be daunting nonetheless.

When we made this decision we were both in our early seventies, and we knew that proceeding down this road would likely be stressful and physically exhausting. Nevertheless, we were confident that the end result - our vision - would make our hard work worthwhile so, after a great deal of research and planning, we moved ahead.

People choose to relocate for a variety of reasons; we had, ourselves, done that very thing on a number of occasions during our lives. This time, though, the rationale for the transition was different for we were deciding who we wanted to be and how we wanted to spend our time. In essence, we were making choices about what mattered most to us at this stage of our lives, and what we wanted our lifestyle to consist of.

And, by the way, describing our move as "rightsizing" rather than "downsizing," is more than a mere exercise in semantics. Simply stated, we were not seeking solely to rid ourselves of unneeded possessions or reduce our footprint on the planet. Our aim was higher; we undertook this move in an effort to craft a lifestyle that would reflect what we were hoping for in our hearts. We were (and are) seeking to be free of home maintenance, to be able to relax, to volunteer, to read, to write, and to live economically. It was our hope that by "rightsizing" our lives in the way this book describes, we would be able to fashion a lifestyle characterized by reduced stress and increased personal contentment.

The pages to follow will detail the various steps we took in making this transition, along with an overview of the different challenges we faced and the manner in which we confronted them. As might be expected, we learned a number of important lessons along the way, and I have outlined them while providing strategies for overcoming difficulties. This book also provides suggestions for dealing with the stress of moving and, at the end, a "Right Sizing Checklist" that helped us make our move more smooth and painless than we ever thought it would be.

I have also included some "post move" thoughts on our level of satisfaction with the new living arrangement in which we find ourselves … spoiler alert … we love it!

When I was a kid, my parents moved a
lot, but I always found them.

Rodney Dangerfield

CHAPTER 1

Moving? Do We
Really Have To?

AFTER MORE THAN FIFTY YEARS of marriage, I had a stock answer
whenever Bonnie suggested we consider moving: "That's between
you and your next husband." In other words, I had no intention
of budging from our home … I was dug in. My very patient wife
usually smiled at my light-hearted comment, for both of us knew
there would be a myriad of things involved in a move, and neither
of us was enthused about starting down that road. And, most especially, at our age.

Over the years we have owned several houses in both New York
and Texas, and we always bought into the notion that owning a
home was part of the American dream. Our three children were
all raised in one or another of those places and, once they were
all moved out and on their own, we "down sized" to a smaller
residence in a lovely community. We were blessed with wonder-
ful neighbors, and a location that gave us easy access to a range of

arts, dining and big-league sporting events. This idyllic setting, we thought, would be the perfect place for us to live out our years.

But time has a way of catching up with people and houses alike. Though perfectly sized, our home was on two levels, and we eventually noticed that we weren't visiting the upstairs rooms as often as we used to ... the stairs were becoming increasingly difficult to climb. With aging, of course, comes the increased risk of a fall, meaning that those attractive wood floors we had installed several years ago made us increasingly nervous; they could be slippery, and a fall on that sort of hard surface would not be cushioned by any carpeting.

Our house was just over thirty years old and, though it was in excellent condition, there always seemed to be some sort of maintenance or housekeeping issue to be taken care of. I had always prided myself on being able to handle most repairs and renovations that came my way, but I had to admit that as I have gotten older I no longer relished the prospect of setting up and climbing an extension ladder to clean the gutters or repair a piece of loose trim. Even keeping up with things on the inside had become daunting. Our home had vaulted ceilings, for example, and something as simple as changing a bulb in a recessed light fixture was not something I looked forward to.

Though the city in which we lived was quite large, the smaller neighborhood that surrounded our home had always been relatively sedate and traffic-free. But over time, the housing boom and associated influx of new residents to our area made driving difficult and a trip to the grocery store had become a chore. Seemingly endless highway construction projects could not keep up with the increased numbers of cars, and we had taken to staying home rather than trying to drive to restaurants and entertainment venues that we had always enjoyed.

Perhaps Bonnie was right ... maybe it was time to think about a new living arrangement.

Once we began to consider moving, though, an entire universe of new questions surfaced. Should we buy another house or should we rent? Ought we to remain in our current area or, perhaps, move to another state? How important would it be to stay near family and friends? Would we be able to find a doctor and other medical specialists who we liked and trusted as much as our current ones? What will we do with all the lovely and meaningful possessions we have accumulated over the years? The list of concerns seemed both endless and daunting.

Bonnie and I are both in our 70's, and we fully understand how a decision of this magnitude can seem overwhelming. For us, though, our ages actually served to stir us to action for, while we both move a bit more slowly than when first married we are, on balance, in good physical and mental shape. That being the case, we felt that a move would best be handled now rather than ten years down the road when we might have to call upon others to manage the process for us. In short, we wanted to be in control of where we would live, how we would make that happen, and when it would occur.

At the risk of sounding impetuous, we both understood that proceeding down this road was, to a certain extent, a "leap of faith." And while we would be making a decision for which the outcome was not entirely certain, we did not move ahead without considerable research and inquiry. After all, in our five decades together, Bonnie and I have made several successful leaps of faith ... when I left college to become a police officer ... when we moved across the country for a new job ... and, of course, entering into marriage is, itself, a leap of faith for any couple.

Naturally, the choices we made and the ultimate outcome of our journey may not be the same for everyone. As they say down at the car dealership, "Your mileage may vary!"

The first step toward getting somewhere is to decide that you are not going to stay where you are.

UNKNOWN

CHAPTER 2

Making The Decision

Once we decided to consider the possibility of moving, we faced a range of issues. Among the most immediate were, first, should we rent or buy and, second, were we going to stay in the general vicinity where we currently resided or would we relocate. Needless to say, each question we considered led directly to a number of additional ones.

Buying Versus Renting

One of the factors that heavily influenced our decision to move into an apartment was the ongoing need for maintenance and other such "home ownership" things in our current place. Our home was in excellent condition, but structures, over time, always seem to need some degree of sprucing up or repair. We lived in a very nice community governed by an excellent HOA, so there was always the necessity to maintain the appearance at a satisfactory level. For example, all of the homes in our neighborhood had stucco exteriors, which meant that every five years or so it was necessary to have the exterior painted.

Owning a home also brought with it concerns about potential damage to the building itself. We live in a part of the country that experiences frequent strong storms and, very often, large hail. In a previous home we sustained extensive roof and glass damage on two occasions and, even though insurance covered most of the repair cost, the stress level and angst that accompanied those two events were considerable. The home we were about to sell had a tile roof and two skylights, so every time storms headed our way I crossed my fingers and hoped that we would be spared.

Renting, on the other hand, was an arrangement that we had not considered for almost fifty years. Owning a home provided the autonomy to paint, landscape or refurbish any way we liked (within HOA limits, of course), but we wondered how well we would adapt to the restrictions imposed by a lease. Needless to say, neighbor noise can be an issue in any living arrangement, but how comfortable would we be with people living above, below and directly on either side of us? Finally, our home had a two-car garage, and hailstorms were always a concern for vehicles as well; what sort of parking arrangement would be available in an apartment setting?

Our financial advisor blanched when we mentioned that we might be considering a move to a rental property versus owning our home. He reminded us of the range of very attractive financing options available for home purchase, and especially those for seniors. We were fortunate to have resided in an area that experienced steady increases in home valuation, so we were confident that the sale of our home would result in our receiving a certain amount of equity at closing. This, of course, raised another question: what would we do with that money if we chose to not buy another house?

Finally, we met and talked with the accountant who prepares our taxes each year. We were interested in his opinion on the renting versus home ownership question, especially since owning a home provides a tax deduction for mortgage interest and taxes. In short, we wanted to know how selling our home and then renting might affect us when it came to filing our Federal income tax. He pointed out that the deductions associated with owning a home are not always the best choice for married couples who file jointly (like us), and that the standard deduction is often a better deal. It is, of course, impossible to predict how income and tax figures might come together at the end of a year but, to us, it seemed like renting would not have a dramatic effect.

LOCATION, LOCATION, LOCATION

A number of very enticing out-of-state options beckoned, and we visited several lovely communities that offered a range of recreational and leisure activities in scenic areas. But each of these places offered few rental options, and buying a home would not satisfy our quest to eliminate home maintenance and upkeep. Any move requires that mailing addresses, government records and contact information be updated, but moving to a different state would present a range of additional administrative tasks such as obtaining new driver licenses and vehicle registrations. And one more very important point: our current state does not tax personal income, while each of the other locations we considered would do so.

When we moved to Texas from New York almost thirty years ago, only our youngest daughter made the transition with us; our two oldest were already out on their own. Over the years, though, all three of our children have taken up residence within an hour or so of where we live. And since each of them is now married with children, the importance of staying relatively close to them - and to our grandchildren - had to be carefully considered.

An additional factor to consider, of course, was that of aging. Although we are both relatively healthy and mobile, there could come a time when we might need to call upon our children for assistance. That being, the case, it seemed to make sense to us that we seriously consider remaining fairly close to where our extended family is located. There is, of course, never a guarantee that one or another of our children might not decide to move elsewhere; we had, after all, done exactly that several times in the course of our married life.

Incidentally, this last point helped tilt us toward renting and the mobility that comes with freedom from home ownership for, much like our children, we could decide to move at some point as well. Our current lease, for example, is for one year and though we expect to stay where we are presently situated, we could decide eventually that new surroundings or a move to a different state might be agreeable. In such a case, rather than having to go through the ritual (and stress) of listing and selling a house again, we could simply pack up and move at the end of the lease.

COST OF RENTING VERSUS HOME OWNERSHIP

In order to determine whether our finances would be adequate to rent a suitable home or apartment, we tried to be as inclusive as possible in calculating expenses for each. To help us do so, we developed two lists:

Home Ownership Expenses:

Mortgage
Taxes
Electric Service
Water, Sewer, Trash pickup
HOA Fees (Neighborhood)
HOA Fees (Community)
TV/Internet/Phone
Quarterly pest control
Heat/AC service contract
Alarm Company Fees
Regular landscaping

Rental Expenses:

Monthly Rent
Utilities
TV/Internet/Phone

Shortly after we contracted with a realtor (more on that in the next chapter), she gave us a homework assignment that proved to be a genuine eye-opener in terms of identifying the true cost of owning a home. She directed us to walk around our home and list every renovation or repair we had undertaken since we owned it and ... Wow! When we tallied up the amount we had spent on a broad range of things over the sixteen years we had lived in our home, we were astounded.

In recent years, for example, we had (among other things) installed a patio in the backyard ... replaced the heat and AC unit ... painted the exterior of the house (twice) ... put up a new wood fence ...planted landscape shrubs ... installed wood floors throughout ... upgraded the kitchen. For us, at least, these expenditures were essentially "sunk costs" which we tended to overlook in any discussion of the true expense of home ownership. Needless to say, looking at these projects through the prism of our realtor's exercise was very revealing.

Content that we had performed due diligence before moving ahead, we decided two things: first, we would rent rather than buy and, second, we would remain in the larger geographic region where we had lived for the past three decades.

It's easier to die than to move … at least
for the Other Side you don't need trunks.

WALLACE STEGNER

CHAPTER 3

Finding A New Abode

WHEN WE BEGAN TO EXAMINE options for renting, we came to understand the old axiom: "So many choices … so little time." We had not yet listed our home for sale, of course, so we did not feel particularly rushed. But as a plethora of attractive rental choices quickly came before us, it was clear that we would be wise to act quickly in narrowing down our options else we risked being overtaken by analysis paralysis (a condition in which someone overthinks a situation to the point where no decision is ever made).

Early in the process, we established a "wish list" of things that we hoped our new living arrangement would offer:

- ❀ Quiet
- ❀ Security
- ❀ Welcoming to seniors
- ❀ At least two bedrooms and two baths
- ❀ Easily accessible medical care

* Relatively close to shopping
* A church in the neighborhood
* Secure covered parking for two vehicles
* Minimal traffic congestion
* Reasonable rent

REGIONAL FACTORS

Since traffic and congestion were among the forces driving us to consider a new housing arrangement, it was important that we find something where those sorts of issues were less of a problem. At one point we had considered the possibility of renting a loft or a center-city place where we would have access to mass transit and could walk to entertainment and dining. For us, though, the difficulty in such a setting would be access to grocery shopping and other such services, and the high rental costs for suitable space were deal breakers.

Wanting to stay relatively close to children and grandchildren, we explored locations on the outer edges of larger metropolitan areas in our region and found a number of interesting choices. Traffic was, generally, less congested in those areas, and each was only a very short jaunt to the rural areas that have always enjoyed driving through and visiting. In addition, being on the edge of major communities would give us access to city services, shopping and entertainment, while insulating us from the increasing traffic jams that we were working to avoid.

For many years, we enjoyed outstanding care through one particular medical group and were, naturally, interested in associating with doctors and hospitals able to approximate that same level of service in our new neighborhood. Like most seniors, this was a very important point for us. For a number of years we owned a cabin on a small lake in East Texas which we thought might serve as our ultimate retirement home. Unfortunately, it was a 45 minute drive to the nearest hospital so, knowing this would not suffice in an emergency, we had no choice but to sell that lovely place.

As we began to narrow our choices we were very pleased to learn that the group of physicians with whom we had such a positive long term relationship actually had a branch close to one of the neighborhoods in which we were interested, and the hospital district was less than a ten minute drive. It was a relief to know we might be able to stay with the same medical practice for, among other positives, access to all of our records would be seamless and instantaneous. For obvious reasons, this fact weighed very heavily in the final choice we made.

Church is an essential element in our lives as well. Our home had been situated within a large parish in which we were very comfortable, and we hoped that our search would put us in a place near a congregation that would allow us to feel equally at home. As luck would have it, the area that we found near to our desired medical practice (mentioned above) was also very close to a lovely church that offered a number of ways to become involved within a very caring community. To be able to check this important item off our list meant a great deal to us.

Types of Rental Properties

Privately Owned Homes Though some were located in very attractive settings, the concern we had with this sort of rental was that of permanence. It was our intention to find a place that we liked and then rent it on a long term basis, and we knew we would be uneasy about what the property owner might choose to do with the home over time. Would he, for example, decide to put the house up for sale? Could the landlord decide that he wanted to move back into the house himself? We certainly did not want to settle in to a place that we liked, only to find that we had to pack up and move on short notice.

Continuing Care Retirement Communities We looked at a number of interesting senior living facilities that offered a range of all-inclusive services such as independent living, assisted living and nursing home care. In this sort of place, a resident would - on one campus - be able to age in place, and receive care based on needs that change over time. In this type of housing, meals and local transportation are typically provided, and a broad menu of activities is available. While attractive, we decided against this sort of a community for two reasons: first, this type of graduated care is very expensive and, second, we did not feel that we needed (at least at this point) the levels of extended care these places offer.

Traditional Apartment Complexes The population in our area had grown significantly over the past few years, and lovely apartment complexes seemed to spring up on a weekly basis. While most appeared to be targeted either at younger professionals or families with children, we decided to visit several to determine what kind of a fit they might be. To us, the "trendier" places offered amenities and a "vibe" that were more suitable for younger folks, and family oriented complexes were aimed at, well, families. Since a quiet environment was high on our list of "wants," we did not think either of these options would meet our needs.

Over-55 Active Retirement Communities Bonnie and I are both innately skeptical when it comes to product advertising. That being the case, it should come as no surprise that we were doubtful when we came across Active Retirement Communities that described themselves using terms such as spacious maintenance-free apartments, designer living, fun activities, clubs, social outings and resort-inspired services. These sorts of places might exist, we thought, but we were certain they would not fit our needs or, especially, be in our price range.

When we visited several of these places, though, we were both amazed and impressed. Clearly, someone had identified a "niche market" of folks, who, like us wanted to be safe and comfortable in affordable surroundings, and then designed communities to fit those needs. While we still had a number of questions that needed answers, it looked like we might have found the sort of living arrangements we were seeking. Now we just had to find the exact over-55 retirement community in which we believed we would be most comfortable.

Welcome Home

After touring several age-restricted over-55 communities in our larger region, we settled upon a lovely apartment community about forty miles from our current home that seemed to meet our needs very well. Located on the outer, largely residential, edge of a city that we always enjoyed visiting, this relatively new place was almost fully occupied; there was only one apartment available in the configuration that interested us. Before meeting with the rental agent, we made sure to peruse the surrounding area and check on the availability of the various amenities we knew we would require. When it came time to seal the deal for the apartment, we were very pleased with what our new apartment home would offer:

- Age-restricted 55 and over
- Two bedrooms and two full baths
- Square footage virtually identical to our home
- Water, electric and trash removal included in rent
- We control our own thermostat
- All appliances included
- 24 hour emergency maintenance
- Secure and gated building and grounds
- Underground parking

- Three elevators
- Outdoor pool, putting green, and walking path
- A menu of available activities for residents
- A guest suite available for visitors
- Church located five minutes away
- Our doctor's office and hospital ten minutes away
- Full assortment of shopping nearby
- Much less traffic than where we were moving from
- Very quiet environment
- Rent within our target range

All that remained was for us to sign the lease, and find a date to move in.

Oh ... and, of course, we had to sell our house.

The Top 10 Things to Do
When Selling Your Home:
#1 Call Me
(I'll handle the other 9)

ADVICE FROM A REALTOR

CHAPTER 4

Selling The Homestead

Setting out to put our house on the market, we felt a surge of confidence from knowing that several homes in our neighborhood had, in the very recent past, sold very quickly at or near the asking price. As a matter of fact, a house just down the street had sold even before it was listed. In that case, someone driving through the area learned that it had just become available, asked to look at it, and bought it immediately. Luckily, the real estate agent who handled that sale had left her business card at nearby houses including ours, so we gave her a call.

For us, meeting with the realtor signified the moment when we both realized that the wheels were now fully in motion, and that this thing was really happening. Up to that point we had been mere window shoppers casually strolling through housing choices at our leisure, but with the signing of a contract we were committed. It was also the first time when little twinges of stress began to creep in; we knew from past experience that buying or selling a home can be highly stressful, but that the right real estate agent can make all the difference. Luckily, the person we selected to guide us through this process was professional, energetic and well-informed. In short, she was excellent!

As an aside, it was interesting to note how many times people, upon learning we were working with a realtor, asked why we didn't just handle the details ourselves. "It's not that hard," they would suggest, "and you can save a lot of money." Um ... well ... did I mention the stress associated with selling or buying a home? We already knew that we had a lot of work ahead of us in getting ready for a sale and then making the actual move, so there was absolutely no way we were going to add even more pressure by attempting to navigate the financial and legal intricacies of the real estate transaction itself. For us, having a real estate agent working on our behalf was worth every dime!

At our first meeting, our realtor proposed an "action plan" for marketing and selling our home. We agreed to put a "Coming Soon" sign on the front lawn in about three weeks, and then she would hold an "Open House" on the following weekend. Waiting this period of time to actually list the house, she suggested, would give us time to do a few cosmetic things around the place that would make the house more marketable. Known as "staging," it would require us to remove a number of our artifacts and collectibles, store some of our numerous wall hangings out of sight, and have someone perform a "deep cleaning" of the interior. We agreed with all that she suggested, so we signed the contract with her and then crossed our fingers in hopes that things would move quickly.

What happened next qualifies as "moving quickly" ... our house sold in less than one day!

Shortly after we signed the contract and the realtor departed, we contacted an acquaintance who had told us to let him know if we ever decided to put our house on the market. When we gave him the news about having listed our home, he asked if he could come by that afternoon to walk through; we, of course, replied in the affirmative. Once he had done so, he asked to return the next morning with his wife so they could look at it together and, once again, we invited him to do so. The next morning they came to our front door, walked through the house, and told us they wanted to buy it. There was no negotiation about a lower number; he offered our asking price and we accepted.

We agreed to contact our respective real estate agents so they could begin formalizing the purchase, and we discussed a potential closing date of just over thirty days in the future. After they departed, we called our realtor with the good news, and then took a moment to reflect on what had just happened. Though absolutely thrilled, we knew that a new set of issues would have to be addressed very quickly. And whereas many "experts" recommend allowing a two to three month time frame from listing to move, ours would take place - assuming all went well - in just over one month.

On the "up" side, we no longer had to plan for an open house. This very common real estate sales practice would have obliged us to "stage" the house and then be absent while strangers walked through our home … this was not something we were enthused about at all, but now it was a non-issue. We were also pleased that we would not have to arrange for temporary storage space for any artwork or furniture from our home that we might have decided to put out of sight in order to make the place look more "open." With the house having sold, it was a relief to know that when we removed items from the walls or shelves it would be for the purpose of actually making ready for the move rather than preparing for showings with potential buyers.

To help us get a sense of which furniture we would move to our new place and which we would dispose of, we returned to the apartment we would be renting and took measurements of each room. We then drew a schematic of the layout, and measured our existing furniture with an eye toward determining how certain pieces might be best arranged in particular areas. Once we went through this exercise we had a much clearer sense of how we would decorate and, more importantly, which of our possessions we would not be taking with us. But as mentioned, the winnowing process for our furniture and numerous other items will be discussed in far greater detail later.

Once the various real estate forms were properly executed, the buyer arranged for a home inspector to conduct a thorough examination of our house. We were certain everything was in very good order, and the inspection report showed that to be the case; only a very few items were identified as needing attention, and we agreed to have them taken care of prior to closing. This was another area in which our realtor proved to be extremely helpful; she provided a list of contractors with whom she had worked in the past, each with a record of professional and reasonably priced work. This list was extremely helpful to us; all of the work was completed in very competent fashion, and the buyer signed off on each item when he did a walk-through before we closed.

To assist the new owner, we made it a point to gather all relevant user manuals and warranties for the several appliances we would be leaving in the house. We also compiled a list of the various service providers and maintenance folks we had come to rely upon over the years. Included in that group were the alarm company we had utilized, the pest control technician who had serviced our home for several years, and the heating/air conditioning group with whom we had a contract for regular system maintenance. When we closed and locked the doors for the last time, we were able to leave behind a good-sized collection of materials that we hoped would be of use to the folks who would be moving in.

Now all we had to do was wait for the closing.

Well, yes, we still had to sort and pack all of our belongings in preparation for the move ... but that wouldn't take long. Would it?

Everybody's gotta have a little place
for their stuff. That's all life is about.
Trying to find a place for your stuff.

George Carlin

CHAPTER 5

Eating the Elephant

Question: How do you eat an elephant?

Answer: One bite at a time.

THIS WELL-KNOWN APHORISM DESCRIBES, PERFECTLY, the approach we decided to take in preparing to move from a house into an apartment. As the euphoria at the sale of our house began to abate, it dawned on us that we had lots of things to do in a very short period of time … and the clock was ticking. But rather than allow events to overwhelm us, we decided to make a list of things that needed to be done, and then accomplish them in methodical, gradual fashion. And at the risk of stereotyping folks our age we decided, first and foremost, to maintain our hallowed tradition of afternoon naps … a decision which proved to be an excellent strategy for keeping us rested, enthused, and focused.

Over the fifty years of our marriage, we had accumulated a lot of "stuff." That being so, our immediate task would be to sort through our possessions and determine which items we would be taking with us to the new place, after which our children would be given the opportunity to take whatever they might like. Finally, the remainder would either be donated to one or another local charity or simply discarded. And while our plan might, at first glance, seem overly cold or clinical, there was a deeply personal element that we knew would weave through the entire process: the memories that many of our heirlooms, souvenirs and other paraphernalia would bring to the surface.

For example, we have travelled extensively during our marriage, and we often made it a point to bring home a poster or print that would remind us where we had been. We would frame and then hang many of them in a room in our house that we used as an office, and the array was both colorful and meaningful. But our apartment, though roomy and nicely laid out, would not accommodate a similar-sized display. So, what to do? We concluded that we both have vivid memories of the many places we visited and a multitude of digital photos, so we felt very comfortable selecting just a few special pictures for display in our new place. Most of the remaining prints were gratefully accepted by our children, or given to neighbors of whom we were fond (and who promised to think of us when they looked at them).

By the way, much of the literature outlining strategies for downsizing or preparing for a move such as ours will recommend having a garage sale. For us, the response to any suggestion of this sort was instantaneous … no way! We have held many garage sales over the years, and we always saw them as a sort of fun way to socialize with neighbors while ridding ourselves of things we no longer needed. But as we worked our way through seemingly endless tasks associated with the move, there was no possibility that we would have either the time or the energy to put price tags on multiple items, collect them in the garage, and then waste a couple of days sitting in the driveway dickering over the price of a snow globe.

According to William Morris, the 17th Century artist and writer, people should: "Have nothing in your houses that you do not know to be useful or believe to be beautiful." With that in mind, we began the process of sorting through and making decisions about our household possessions. For example:

Furniture Knowing that we had more furniture than we would need in our apartment, we took great care to measure the new place, draw a schematic, and check the layout and fit of the furniture we would be bringing to our new digs. Once we decided on the pieces we would be taking, there remained a goodly assortment of furnishings to dispose of. To move the process forward, we took digital photos of the available collection then sent those pictures to each of our children. We also set a date when each of them should consider coming to our house to identify the things they might like. As shall be seen below, the majority of the available items were claimed by our children, and the remaining few pieces were donated to a local charity.

Wall Art As mentioned above, we had a number of prints and posters that we had collected but which would not fit well in our new place. The small assortment that we took with us depicted lovely scenes from New York, our home state, and they had special meaning to us. Our children asked for and were given several others. Incidentally, one of our daughters is a school librarian, and we are pleased that three of those pieces are now on display in her library. Like the excess furniture, any unclaimed prints were donated to charity.

Decorations Several years ago, we went through a "Let's Collect Roosters and Chickens" phase, meaning that we now had more than thirty pieces of various-sized barnyard fowl statuary available for adoption. Each of our children graciously thanked us for offering them those very colorful ceramic, metal and wooden birds, but then steadfastly declined to accept them. Fortunately, the charity donation center was less discerning.

Kitchen Utensils Naturally, our good collection of pots and pans went to the new place, along with an assortment of favorite ovenware. But in cleaning out our kitchen cabinets, we came across a number of odd cookware, utensils and assorted other kitchenware that we had not even seen in years. They were still in good and serviceable shape so, except for the few items our children accepted, those things were donated.

Outdoor Furniture, Equipment and Plants The barbecue grill and patio set from our backyard now reside at our son's house, along with several other outdoor decorative pieces. Bonnie's green thumb had always been in evidence on our patio, but with no similar space in our apartment, our daughters provided good homes for a variety of flowering plants and cacti. Our children also gratefully accepted and divided a variety of tools (both electric and manual) used for trimming and otherwise cleaning up the yard.

Very quickly, we concluded that the most expedient way of approaching this project was to separate our possessions into four categories ... take with ... give away ... donate ... and discard. And just as an aside, we were absolutely ruthless when it came to deciding which items would be placed in which category. As a result, one additional side benefit of this move was the catharsis that flowed from being able to finally free ourselves from storing or hauling around unnecessary baggage that had accumulated over the span of more than fifty years of marriage.

TAKE WITH

In addition to the furniture and other household goods mentioned above we, of course, took the usual assortment of possessions instrumental to daily life: clothing, linens, towels and the like. And since we were moving, we decided to use the occasion to purchase two new beds (a king and a queen); both existing mattresses were in need of replacement, and we were interested in new frames and headboards as well. We had the new beds delivered and assembled in our house about one week before we moved; that way, the delivery team from the furniture store would remove and dispose of our old mattresses, box springs and bed rails. About one week later, the movers assembled the new beds in our apartment, thereby eliminating the hassle of us having to obtain news beds and then remove the old items after completion of the move.

Knowing which pieces of furniture would be used in the apartment gave us the opportunity to decide which of our many pieces of table art, decorations and other "pretties" we would putting on display. Similarly, we planned in advance for the placement of the various lamps or desk lights we would require; this process was made much easier by the fact that each room in the apartment had a ceiling fan and light. Finally, we limited our display of framed pictures of our grandchildren; we have numerous digital and printed photos of the family, so paring down the number on actual display helped make our new place look more "open."

Our new apartment provides a separate storage closet just down the hall, so we were able to bring items like our Christmas decorations and luggage and then store them away from our living space. As will be mentioned below, the relatively small storage room proved more than adequate after we cleared out much of the detritus from our garage and attic.

GIVE AWAY

Like many couples our age, we prepared for marriage by selecting a pattern for a set of formal china and crystal, and picking a design for our "good silverware." And though that tradition seems to have faded away, we had continued to carry (unused) those anachronistic table settings with us over the years. Occasionally, we would offer those lovely items to each of our children, only to have them politely decline to take them off our hands. For that reason, we did not know what to expect when we announced that we had set a firm date to move, and then invited our family to come to the house and identify any items they would like to have.

Unlike the rejection of our formal dinnerware, though, we were pleasantly surprised that interest in our excess furniture and other household goods was very high. As part of the "Stake Your Claim" process we gave each of our children a different colored pad of "sticky notes," and let them tag the items they wanted. Once completed, we set convenient times for them to come and pick them up. We were especially gratified that several important family heirlooms are now safely placed and on loving display in the homes of people who are important to us.

For example, in the 1920s, my grandfather built a lovely wooden cabinet with glass doors. I had inherited this piece and carried it with us through several moves but, sadly, there was no place for it in our apartment. It was my hope that I would be able to hand it off to someone who knew of its history, and would care for it as

I had over the years. Fortunately, our son gladly accepted it, where it is now a perfect fit with the other furnishings in his home!

Speaking of my grandfather, he was highly skilled craftsman with a sizable collection of tools that were handed down to me when he passed away. This was a man who meant a great deal to me, and every time I had the occasion to use one of his tools I thought of him. Needless to say, we would not be needing an extensive assortment tools in our apartment, though I did assemble a tool box of things that might come in handy for hanging curtains or other minor tasks. As to the remainder of my grandfather's tools, I was able to divide them between my son and son-in-law who will put them to continued good use.

DONATE

When it came time to deal with the "donation" category, we were absolutely amazed at the enormous quantity and variety of articles that still remained in our house. We had, after all, identified the things we would be taking with us, and given many other items to our children … so where could all this "stuff" have possibly come from?

Our minivan, which is equipped with back seats that fold flat to the floor, proved to be extremely helpful as we went about carrying our excess goods to the donation center. When we took our first full load, a very nice volunteer helped me unload things at the drop-off door. The next day, we went back to the same donation center with another full load at which point this same volunteer said with some surprise: "It looks like we have your whole house!" Indeed, it did.

In a world where we are all participants in the common marketplace known as the Internet, a number of options exist for making a few dollars selling things online. With moving day rapidly approaching, though, we had no interest in listing things for sale on sites like Craigslist, Ebay or NextDoor, and then having to deal with sales transactions. Instead, we took pictures of each load (for tax purposes), and picked up a receipt for our contribution. Yes, any tax benefit for this sort of thing is negligible, but we were comforted that our small donation would have some potential benefit to someone in need. And, of course, the primary goal was to be rid of things that we would not be taking to our apartment.

DISCARD

We were fortunate that our house was in a city with an outstanding solid waste department, so most of what we discarded was picked up in their regular rounds. And while we did not have an overabundance of things to throw away, we were glad to be rid of old holiday decorations, odd scraps of lumber, empty plastic containers, faded artificial plants and the like.

And speaking of the solid waste department, they offered an important service that we made certain to call upon. In cleaning out the garage, we collected a number of half-empty paint cans, lawn chemicals and other such substances that cannot be discarded in the same fashion as ordinary trash. For those sorts of things, the city arranged for a special truck to come to the house and remove them for us.

We also used the move as an opportunity to rid ourselves of a wealth of accumulated files and assorted paperwork. Some were tax-related documents from many years back (which did not need to be retained any longer), while others were simply old receipts, work orders, expired warranties and the like. After we had collected the items we no longer wanted, we took them to a commercial shredder where we could watch them being destroyed.

OF SPECIAL NOTE

As we were wrapping up this part of the pre-move preparation, we gave special attention to two important sets of materials:

Legal Documents and Tax Records We took considerable care to protect and retain things that have special importance in our lives and the lives of our children. This would include our wills, for example, along with various Powers of Attorney that we have had prepared and set aside for when the time comes to utilize them. In addition, the IRS recommends retaining tax records for varying lengths of time depending on the circumstances, so we made certain to keep those as well. And rather than trusting these important documents to a mover, we made sure to transport them ourselves on moving day.

Family Photographs As one might imagine, a couple married for more than fifty years will accumulate a sizable trove of photographs. And it goes without saying that the number of prints will increase exponentially with the addition of three children and seven grandchildren over that time. This was the situation at our house … lots and lots of photographs.

Several years ago we sorted through most of this collection, and put together three good-sized sets … one for each of our children. Each grouping contained shots of them over the years, along with family photos that we thought they might enjoy. Doing this helped diminish slightly the overall bulk of pictures, but it did not solve our immediate problem: what should we do with the remainder? Many of the pictures were old and, in fact, the identities of some of those in the photos were, sadly, unknown. We have a number of picture albums that we treasure and with which we will not part, but we simply came to the conclusion that we could no longer continue to store this mountainous collection of miscellaneous snapshots.

In hopes of solving this dilemma, we laid our concerns before our children. We told them that we were no longer going to continue as caretakers of these photos and, if nobody was willing to take custody of them, we would be discarding them. Much to our relief, our two daughters agreed to divide the lot between them, and thus become custodians of this bit of family history.

And, so, with the sorting and winnowing process completed, we were ready for the movers to do their magic.

If I'd known how much packing I'd
have to do, I'd have run again.

HARRY S. TRUMAN

CHAPTER 6

Getting a Move On

WHEN WE WERE YOUNGER, MOVING from one home to another was a fairly simple process: pack belongings in old cardboard boxes from the A&P, rent a truck, line up friends and family to help, provide some beer, and pray that nobody sustained an injury and none of our possessions got broken. Today, though, things are considerably more complicated as friends and family have gotten older and, thus, less willing/able to help, while those still in their prime "furniture moving" years have become (rightly) less eager to sacrifice their weekend in exchange for a sore back and a couple of warm brews.

As for me, I knew my days as a mover were over years ago when a friend asked if I could help him move some furniture in his house. When I got to his place I learned that the "furniture" was an upright piano with a lead sounding board, and that he wanted it moved upstairs. Looking at the other three "volunteers" my friend had invited, I noticed we all had several things in common … we were young … we were big … and we were (presumably) strong.

The piano, though, was the ultimate "immovable object," and we struggled mightily to get that REALLY HEAVY thing up the curved staircase. We finally succeeded with only a few minor abrasions, some damaged wall board and a broken railing, but I learned a valuable lesson that day: when it comes to moving, it is worth paying a few bucks to professionals who know what they are doing.

Choosing the Right Company

And so, keeping in mind our goal of effecting this move with as little stress as possible, we set out to find a suitable moving company. Very quickly, though, this seemingly simple quest resulted in "information overload" as we found ourselves sorting through an extraordinary number of moving companies advertising on the Internet and elsewhere. Nationally known conglomerates … local crews who seemed to operate on a shoestring … fire fighters with trucks … mom and pop operations … the list went on. Finally, we decided to explore two options that appeared to offer services that came the closest to what we were looking for: the first were senior relocation specialists, and the second were concierge movers who would "do it all" for us.

Senior Relocation Specialists A relatively new specialty, professionals in this area provide a broad range of services to the over-55 segment of society. As we met with and interviewed several companies, we were impressed by the obvious attention to detail they promised in handling the entire move process for us. They would, for example, take pictures of our current room arrangements and decorations, and then set up our new place so it would look virtually identical.

As we talked further, it was clear that the services offered by these groups would be ideal and much-sought-after in circumstances where clients with physical or mental limitations (or their families) could be assured that every detail of a move would be handled with care and grace. Some of what these groups offer, in fact, would likely be especially reassuring to someone who, even in the face of necessity, might be reluctant to move after many years in one home. While impressive in scope we did not feel that, at this point in our lives, we would require the range of services offered by organizations of this sort.

Concierge or "Do It All" Services In researching local moving companies we noticed one, in particular, with a Better Business Bureau rating of A+ and a number of very positive customer reviews. We spoke with their representative who explained the very reasonable per-hour cost for packing, moving and unpacking us, along with a range of other "concierge" services that we could consider if necessary. Those extra services included such things as arranging for change of address notifications, handling the details for any donations to be picked up, and setting up junk removal if necessary. All in all, our reaction to the reputation of this company and what they offered was ... wow!

As we dug deeper, we found there was a lot to like about this fully licensed, insured and bonded moving company, not the least of which was their screening and training of uniformed staff. We were attracted, as well, to their promise of care and concern for us and our personal needs, and we learned that we would have a "move coordinator" as our point of contact throughout the process.

Though the range of available "add-on" services was impressive, we would require only the packing of our goods beforehand, the actual move itself, and unpacking of our things in our new place. We decided to contract with this local concierge moving company, and we are very glad that we did. Their service was excellent, and the resultant stress-free process of transporting everything from point A to point B was flawless.

Making the Move

On the day before our actual move, two men arrived at our home at 9:00am, fully prepared to get all of our possessions boxed, cushioned, disassembled and otherwise ready for loading and transporting the next day. The company provided all the cardboard cartons, paper and bubble wrap (for which we paid), and we provided direction on what needed to be boxed and how things should be marked for proper placement in our apartment. We had already "pre-packed" certain collectibles and other delicate items, but the moving men wrapped, cushioned and boxed all dishes and glassware from the kitchen cabinets and our china closet. In short, everything at risk of breaking or being damaged was carefully wrapped, boxed and made ready for transport.

We had made arrangements to spend the night in an area hotel, so we had a suitcase with our clothing and other overnight things already packed. The remainder of our clothes were placed in wardrobe boxes, with the exception of items in the drawers of three dressers; those pieces of furniture were very sturdy, so the movers simply padded and wrapped them with the contents still inside. The beds were disassembled, padded and wrapped, and each piece of furniture we were taking with us was similarly prepared and protected. By the end of the day, everything was in place and ready to go.

At 8:00 am the next morning, the moving truck pulled up in front of our house and things got rolling right away. Whereas only two men had packed and prepared our belongings the day before, the move itself employed three men ... and they moved quickly! Our mission during the loading process was simply to stay out of the way, and to pull together the things that we would be carrying in our car (more on that in a moment). When everything was aboard the truck, we walked through the now-empty house with the move coordinator to make sure everything had been accounted for, after which we set out for the new place.

In that the movers were being paid by the hour (at a very reasonable rate), we were impressed by how quickly they transported everything the forty miles from our house to our apartment. As a matter of fact, even though we left the old neighborhood before the truck, they arrived at the new place before we did. The reason for this was simple: we stopped long enough to pick up a coffee at a Starbucks, and those few moments in the drive through lane were sufficient for them to pass us!

Our apartment is on the second floor and, fortunately, the elevator is only about twenty feet from our front door. Management had reserved the elevator for our use on that day, thereby allowing the movers to have unrestricted access for the duration of the move-in. The work began quickly and, like the loading process, the unloading and unpacking went better than we had any right to expect. The moving crew assembled the beds, unpacked all the dishes, put all of our clothes on the racks in the closets and carried certain items to the storage closet in a separate part of the building. And on an especially happy note, we were pleased that the time spent measuring floor space and furniture paid off, as everything fit perfectly in the areas we had planned.

As they went about cleaning up, the movers asked if we wanted to keep any of the now-empty boxes and wrapping materials we had paid for. We had no interest in (or space for) retaining any, so we declined the offer with assurances that the collection would be properly recycled. With the move coordinator we did a walk through of our now-fully-furnished place, and verified that nothing was broken or missing. The movers, having spent only eight hours to load, move, unload and unpack us, departed with our thanks for a job very well done.

OF SPECIAL NOTE

While the moving company and its staff did a commendable job moving our possessions safely and securely, there were certain items that we chose to transport ourselves on moving day. For example, sensitive documents to include our Wills and Powers of Attorney were hand-carried to our new address, along with our computer and similar electronic equipment. Naturally, we made sure to back up all files before disconnecting the computer and placing it in our car. We also transported food from our pantry, along with refrigerated and frozen goods. Finally, we carried with us an assortment of houseplants.

Part of the reason for us transporting these items ourselves was our concern for the absolute security of certain things. For other items, though, moving companies are prohibited by federal law from transporting them. A list of articles moving companies are barred from carrying would include hazardous materials like propane, ammunition and other flammable items, along with lawnmowers and gas grills. Similarly, moving companies will not move perishable things like food and plants. We had educated ourselves about these restrictions so, on moving day, there was no last minute confusion about what the movers would take and what we would have to transport on our own.

When we laid out the time line for our pre-move preparation and the move itself, we factored in one additional day at the end that would allow us to return to our house and do a full cleaning of the premises. This was a bittersweet process, for this very comfortable house had meant a great deal to us for more than sixteen years, and we wanted to be sure that we left it in pristine condition for the new owners. We were pleased that we were able to do so.

And with that ... we were done!

Where we love is home - home that our
feet may leave, but not our hearts.

Oliver Wendell Holmes

CHAPTER 7

And The Verdict Is ....

IT HAS BEEN A BUSY few months but, overall, we are now settled in well at our new apartment. We've had the chance to meet many of our neighbors, the local streets are no longer a maze, and we have found a goodly number of places to do our shopping. We are getting our hair cut and gassing up the cars at familiar and comfortable places, and Bonnie has found a nail salon she likes … meaning all is good!

So, what do we think? Was this move a good thing for us? Would we have done anything differently?

Readers will recall us tipping our hand with the answer to that question in the Introduction to this book but, without question, this has been an excellent decision. We understand, of course, that life can throw curves at any time and that, six months down the road, we may find our living arrangement not nearly as pleasant as it currently seems to be. But the horizon looks clear, and we are enjoying our new lifestyle to the fullest.

Perhaps a brief Q & A will help to illustrate how things have turned out:

How long did this entire exercise take? Once we started to think seriously about the possibility of moving, it was approximately three months until we waved goodbye to the last mover as he exited the door of our new apartment. As mentioned in Chapter 4, our house sold very quickly and, as a consequence, the time to close and physically move was compressed far more than usual. While this abbreviated time line could have been a stress inducer, we made certain to handle things in careful, deliberate fashion, while taking care to relax and decompress along the way.

Are you still in touch with friends in the old neighborhood? Of course. A number of our former neighbors are good friends, and those friendships remain vibrant. Many have been by to visit our new place, and we make it a regular practice to stop and chat with them when we are in the area where we used to reside. Email, of course, is an excellent way to maintain strong lines of communication today and we use it regularly.

Have you connected socially in your new place? It has been enjoyable to find ourselves in an environment with folks close in age to our own. The over-55 community where we live has a number of social opportunities to choose from, and our new neighbors have been extremely warm and welcoming. There is no pressure to participate in any particular activities, and we have settled comfortably into several groups with interests similar to our own. We were also delighted to learn of the many volunteer opportunities nearby to us, and have begun spending time assisting at a local food pantry.

Is your apartment complex safe and secure? We feel very safe and at ease here. The exterior doors are kept locked, and visitors use a touchpad that connects to our apartment from which we can open the door remotely. Our vehicles are parked in an underground garage with gates that can only be opened using a key fob. In terms of emergency services, we are located within a city that provides excellent police, fire and ambulance service, and the hospital district is only a very few minutes away.

How does the new neighborhood compare with the old? Both areas are very attractive and well-maintained, but our new location has far fewer traffic problems. Reduced traffic congestion was on our "wish list" when we began our quest, so we are pleased that we found that sort of a setting in the midst of a largely residential zone on the outer edge of a good-sized city we have long enjoyed. We also hoped to find a church relatively nearby, and we were successful in that. As a matter of fact, we now live closer to our parish than ever before in our married lives.

Did you have to do any work on the apartment before moving in? Our complex provides a certain amount of free handyman service and, in addition, we were able to select our carpet and make several other choices in kitchen and bath design. Beyond that, we hired a contractor to install drapery rods prior to moving in. We wanted the move to be as comfortable and seamless as possible, and we felt that the "settling in" process would be enhanced by having curtains already hung on the first day. Later, we hired that same contractor to install several ceiling fans in rooms that did not have them initially.

Was it difficult to update government records with the new address? Since most government entities now have robust web sites, the process is smooth and user friendly. As a matter of fact, many agencies actively encourage citizens to make changes electronically. Things like voter registration, driver licenses, Medicare and Social Security were all handled electronically, with updated documents received or confirmed within two to three weeks. For those who enjoy standing in line to meet with a government employee, that option still exists. For the rest of us, though, handling this chore on the web is the way to go.

What was the most difficult part of this process? The most time-consuming and physically tiring part was the winnowing and packing process for our possessions. As mentioned elsewhere, we had accumulated a lot of "stuff," and we made it our goal to reduce that conglomeration as much as possible. Fortunately, our children helped the process immensely by selecting items that they wanted for their homes; this was uplifting, for it meant that many of the things we had enjoyed would continue on in the lives of people we care about. It was truly refreshing, though, to simply rid ourselves of "stuff" we had been carrying along with us but which no longer had any useful purpose.

Do you miss owning a house? Not even a little bit. One of the primary reasons underlying our decision to move was the desire to be free from maintenance and upkeep issues, and our new apartment has done that for us. We are very comfortable knowing that the resolution of any maintenance issue is only a phone call away. As one of our new neighbors recently said: "When I owned a house and sat on the back porch, all I saw in the yard was things that needed to be done!" We have a good-sized deck at our new place which we have furnished with two rocking chairs and an assortment of lovely flowers; when we sit outside in the evening all we see is the beautiful view.

There is, of course, a universal belief that owning a house is a historic indicator of success, and that those with large homes, high income and lots of toys are even more successful. Perhaps, but each of us has to decide what is most important in life, and then find a meaningful way of measuring how well we live in concert with our goals. As mentioned earlier, the square footage of our apartment is almost identical to the home we sold. That was an interesting coincidence but, to us, layout and location were more important than the size of our dwelling. In the final analysis, we celebrate the fact that we are very comfortable in our new neighborhood, and that we are close to things that are important to us.

In the 1913 children's book, *Pollyanna*, by Eleanor Porter, the main character attempts to find something positive in every situation. Today, a person who always seems to be upbeat despite the circumstances is often described as pollyannish, with the implication that an overly optimistic viewpoint and relentless cheeriness can be taken too far. I mention this simply because in reviewing the pages of this book, I am fearful that some readers might think me a pollyanna in the reporting our experience. Those with unhappy experiences as renters would, perhaps, suggest that I overlooked a number of problems that plague apartment dwellers and they would be correct. As pointed out early on, the purpose here was to outline what our experiences have been and, needless to say, anyone planning a similar change in lifestyle should conduct their own extensive research and ask key questions before starting out. One size does not fit all, after all, and our very positive experience may not transfer perfectly to another couple.

Full disclosure, our experience at the new place has not been entirely blemish free. Before we moved, we made certain to transfer our newspaper subscription from our old address to our new and, for the most part, the change was seamless. The only "glitch" involved the Sunday paper which was not being delivered on time. I contacted the distribution office each week and they made sure it came to our door eventually. Our delivery person, however, eventually left me a note explaining why the paper was late on Sundays. In it, he pointed out that he had a time window in which he had to deliver to "actual residences" on that day and, as a result, he would not be able to deliver as early as usual to our "nursing home."

Nursing home?

One of my all time favorite TV programs is "The Sopranos." And even though it completed its run several years ago I still, every once in a while, watch the entire series on DVD. In one especially memorable episode, Tony Soprano (the mob boss) struggles to relocate his elderly mother, Livia, from her home to a senior living facility known as Green Grove. Wanting no part of the plan, Livia, insists that she will not move there because it is a "Nursing Home!" Frustrated and at the end of his patience, Tony declares with some vehemence: "Ma, it's not a nursing home … it's a retirement community!"

Although I was more polite than Tony Soprano would have been, I explained this fact to our newspaper delivery person.

We live in a retirement community.

And we are loving it.

Don't fear failure so much that you refuse to try new things.
The saddest summary of life contains three descriptions:
could have, might have, and should have.

UNKNOWN

A RIGHTSIZING CHECKLIST

~~⌇~~

THE FOLLOWING LIST IS DRAWN from our personal experience as we went about contemplating and then carrying out the "rightsizing" of our lives in 2017. This assortment of ideas should not be seen as a fully comprehensive collection of items to think about when selling a house and moving; individual circumstances, after all, might (and should) call for special consideration.

1. **Start With The End In Mind** In his book *The 7 Habits of Highly Effective People*, Steven Covey suggests that each of us think about who we are and what we want in life, and then stay focused on the desired outcome. In contemplating a move, we began by imagining what we wanted our new living arrangement and lifestyle to look like, and then worked toward that goal. For us, staying on target was especially important as the clock wound down, and at those occasional times when we became weary or frustrated.

2. **Should We Purchase or Rent?** Should we buy another house, or is it smarter to rent?
   1. What are the tax implications of each?
   2. Do we want to contend with maintenance and upkeep of a house?
   3. Will apartment living be too restrictive for us?
   4. Which choice will best accommodate the lifestyle we are seeking?
   5. Given our financial situation, what is our rent or mortgage ceiling?

3. **Where Do We Want to Live?** How important is location in our choice?
   1. Do we want to stay close to loved ones?
   2. As we get older, will family assistance be necessary?
   3. Is a change of scenery or climate important to us?
   4. If we move to another state, what will be the difference in taxes?
   5. Is public transportation available and easily accessed?

4. **What Are We Looking For In A New Place?** Are there specific things we are seeking in a new residence and neighborhood?
   1. How safe is a given area? What are the crime statistics?
   2. Is there adequate shopping nearby?
   3. What are the traffic and road congestion conditions?
   4. Is there access to sports, dining and entertainment?
   5. Are there educational and volunteer opportunities nearby?

5. **What Level of Medical Care or Assistance Might We Need?** As we get older, will we be able to meet any medical needs associated with aging?
   1. Are there adequate medical facilities and specialists nearby?
   2. If renting, is a "Continuing Care" facility the right choice for us?
   3. Will our home or apartment accommodate handicaps?
   4. Are home health aides available in the area?
   5. Are transportation services available for elderly or handicapped?

6. **How Do We Put Our House On The Market?** What is the best time to list, and how should we determine asking price?
   1. Should we call upon a realtor or do it ourselves?
   2. What sort of preparation will we have to do before the house goes up for sale?
   3. Should we hire a professional service to do a "deep cleaning"?
   4. If we need to "declutter" our home, how should we store excess items?
   5. Are all appliances and similar equipment in good working order?

7. **What Should We Do With All Our "Stuff"?** How best to deal with all the baggage we have accumulated over the years?
   1. Separate into four categories: Take With … Give Away … Donate … Discard
   2. Be ruthless about getting rid of unneeded things

3. How should we deal with "special items" like family heirlooms?

4. Decide on and then measure furniture you will be taking with you

5. Check the fit and arrangement of your things on a schematic of the new place

8. **How Should We Make The Actual Move?** What sort of services are available to help us prepare for and actually perform the move?

1. Do it yourself? Professional movers?

2. Is a Senior Relocation Specialist right for us?

3. Evaluate and check references for the moving company

4. What shall we transport ourselves on moving day?

5. Is the new place ready for our arrival on the appointed day?

9. **Updating, Changing and Closing Out** What government, financial or medical records need to be updated?

1. What services and utilities will we have to cancel at the old place?

2. What services and utilities will we have to start at the new place?

3. Which government documents need to be updated?

4. Address changes for post office, banks and credit cards

5. Update home or renter's insurance

10. **Like Santa … Make A List And Check It Twice!** Despite the "cutesy" heading, this is a critical component undergirding a move like this. At the very beginning, we

compiled a list of things that needed to done and then paid close attention to it as we went through the process. We would check off items as they were completed, and add new things as they came to our attention. Some tasks had to be performed before others, of course, and a comprehensive but flexible list (updated regularly) proved to be essential. Sticking to this list also gave us confidence and a feeling of accomplishment, for we could see that we were actually getting things done!

Finally, it is important to carve out time for rest and relaxation along the way. At the start of an adventure like this, the mountain of tasks and chores associated with moving can seem overwhelming, and one can be left to wonder where to start. And while it may strike some as counterintuitive to formally plan for a nap or other sorts of diversions in the midst of all that needs to be done, the value of setting aside time for rest cannot be overstated. For us, it was essential that we take on this project in small bites and, as we did so, to stay focused on the goal we had set for ourselves … a rightsized life.

ABOUT THE AUTHOR

DAN CARLSON IS A RETIRED law enforcement officer and educator who enjoys writing about things that are near and dear to his heart. He and his wife, Bonnie, reside in the Great State of Texas in close proximity to their three children and seven grandchildren. Dan knows he is a very lucky man.

DanBonBooks.com

OTHER BOOKS BY DAN CARLSON

Dear Hippie … We Met at Woodstock
One Cop's Memories of the 1969 Woodstock Festival
2016, Amazon

Dear Prostate … I Thought You Were My Friend
One Man's Journey Through Prostate Cancer and Beyond
2016, Amazon

When Cultures Clash
Strategies for Strengthening Police-Community Relations
2005, Pearson-Prentice Hall

Reputable Conduct
Ethical Issues in Policing and Corrections
2004, Pearson-Prentice Hall (with Dr. John Jones)